A large PART of the INSPIRATion
For this BOOK came From REPEATEDLy
trying to EXPLAIN the HISTORY and
GEOGRAPHY of the NORThern IRELAND
CONFLICT - to SMART people, who
neither KNEW, not REALLY CARED
ABOUT it — OVER the DISTANCE
of AN OCEAN.

"From out there on the moon, international politics look
so petty. You want to grab a politician by the scruff of the
neck and drag him a quarter of a million miles out and say,
'Look at that...'"

— **Edgar Mitchell,** Apollo 14 astronaut, 1974

"For man, unlike any other thing organic or inorganic in
the universe, grows beyond his work, walks up the stairs
of his concepts, emerges ahead of his accomplishments."

— **John Steinbeck,** *The Grapes of Wrath*, 1939

To Harland and Mari
Future keepers of the peace
(I hope)

PHILOMEL BOOKS
An imprint of Penguin Random House LLC, New York

First published in the United Kingdom by HarperCollins, 2022
First published in the United States of America by Philomel Books,
an imprint of Penguin Random House LLC, 2022

Visit us online at penguinrandomhouse.com.

Library of Congress Cataloging-in-Publication Data is available.

Printed in the USA

ISBN 9780593621523

10 9 8 7 6 5 4 3 2 1

PC

Design by Rory Jeffers

**All calculations made by
astrophysicist Stephen Smartt**

Thank you
Suzanne Jeffers, Fru Czech, David Lewis,
Aaron Ruff, Gabe Benzur, Ben Cady,
Emma Miller, Philippa Jordan,
Ann-Janine Murtagh, Val Brathwaite,
Geraldine Stroud and Edge.

This book is a companion to the art installation
Our Place in Space – an epic scale model of
the solar system. The 10km sculpture trail was
developed by Oliver Jeffers, astrophysicist
Professor Stephen Smartt, and the Nerve Centre
and creative partners, as part of the UNBOXED
program funded by the UK government.

www.ourplaceinspace.earth

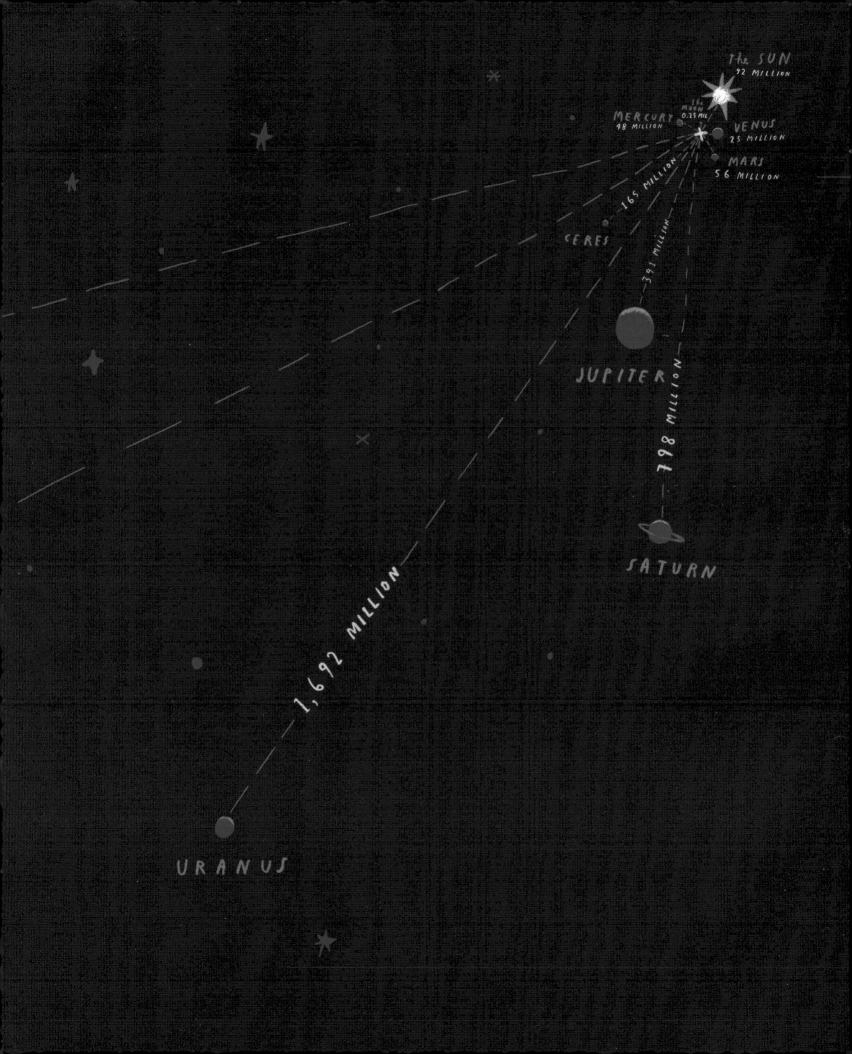

MEANWHILE
BACK ON EARTH...

OLIVER JEFFERS

PHILOMEL

In all of the cosmos . . .

...this one place in our solar system...

...is where all of the people have lived...

for the whole time we've been people.

We have always thought that Earth

is so big . . .

...that it's best to divide it into smaller bits.

It seems we humans ...

...have always fought each other over space.

Though, really, Earth is not so big. Not compared to ...

well, SPACE.

Shall we take a detour and see for ourselves?

Then, let's put on our space helmets …

turn this into a space car . . .

...and head out toward the moon.
It is a quarter of a million miles away so

it will take almost a year to drive there.

(All speeds and distances calculated at 37 mph* – the average speed humans drive at.)

*miles per hour

On this trip it's important to keep checking the mirror
to see what we're up to back on Earth.

So ... if we were already at the moon,
it would be almost a year ago at home.

And we'd see Earth much as we left it
at the start of the twenty-first century,

where everyone seems distracted
and can't agree what we do next.

If we took a left turn at the moon (toward the sun), it would be a
seventy-eight-year drive from Earth to Venus – our closest planet.

Meanwhile back on Earth,
seventy-eight years ago,

it was the middle of the twentieth century...

and the whole planet was fighting –
hopefully for the last time.

Meanwhile back on Earth, 150 years ago,
it was late in the 1800s, and...

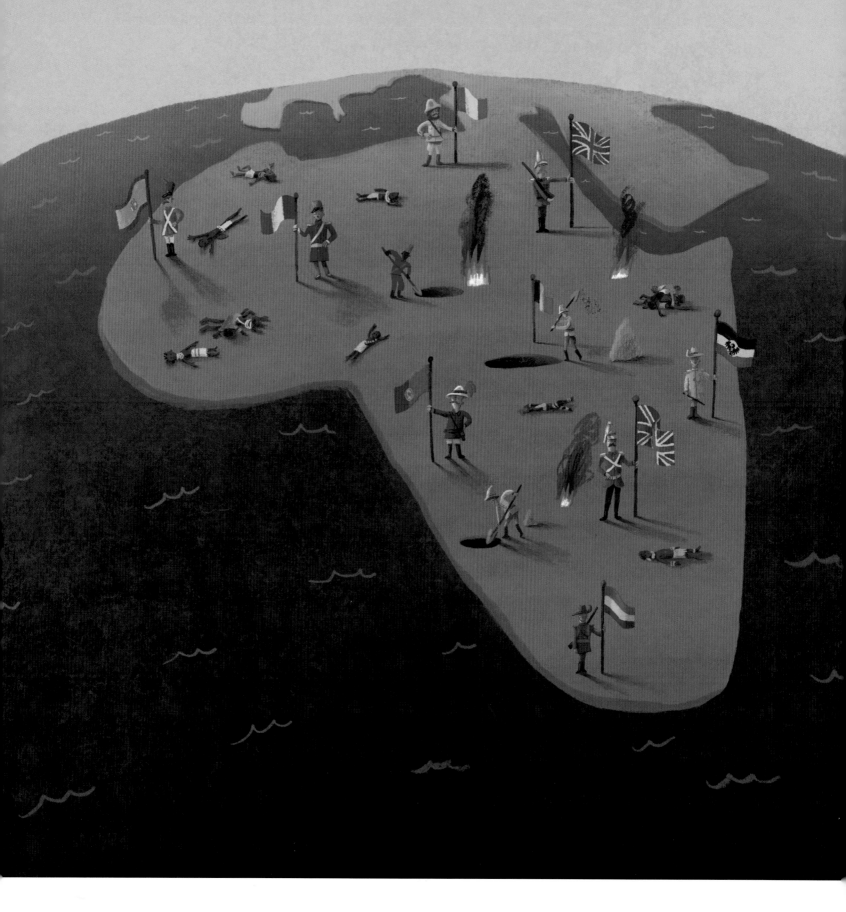

a few small countries were racing to divide up and
own a valuable bit of land and the people in it.

If, back at the moon, we made a right turn
(instead of a left)

and headed toward Mars,
it would take about 170 years to get there.

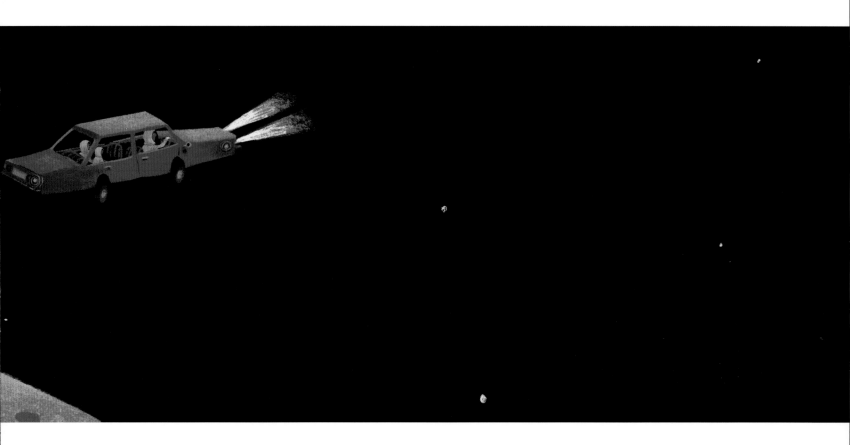

Meanwhile back on Earth, 170 years ago,
it was the middle of the 1800s

and four different empires were fighting over a small bit of land

that stuck out into a small sea.

Back on our original course, it would be a 283-year drive to reach the sun.

(Make sure you have the air-conditioning going, and your sunglasses on.)

Meanwhile back on Earth,
283 years ago, it was the middle of the 1700s

and some humans

(after sailing across an ocean and fighting with the humans who were already there)

were about to start fighting each other.

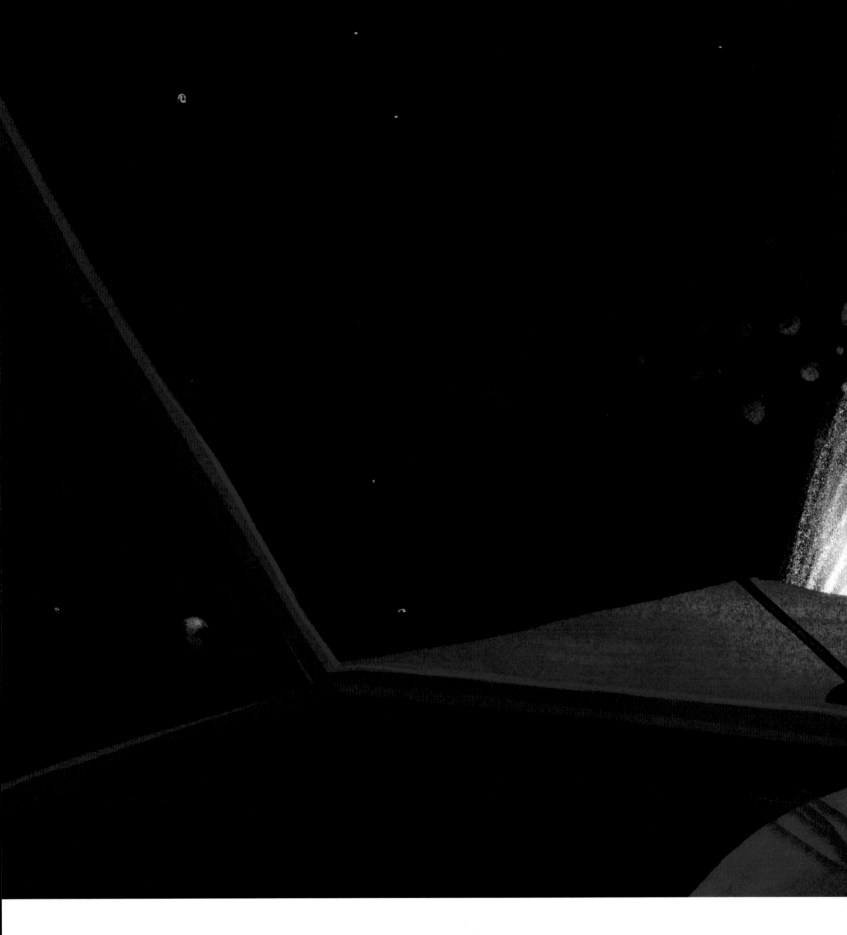

Now, if we'd made that right turn toward Mars, and kept going,
we would be driving for 500 years, from Earth, before we saw anything else.

When we eventually did, it would probably be
Ceres, the largest object in the asteroid belt.

Checking in the year-view mirror,
we see that back on Earth, 500 years ago,

the first people from one big bit of land
arrived at the other big bit of land and ran riot.

I hope you're comfortable (and brought snacks),
as it takes almost 1,200 years to drive to Jupiter.

Back on Earth, 1,200 years ago,
it was the year 800 (and something),

and the Vikings had finished fighting everyone around them,
so they built boats to find new people to fight.

But let's keep going,

as it's only a short 2,400-year drive to Saturn.

Meanwhile back on Earth, two and a half millennia ago,

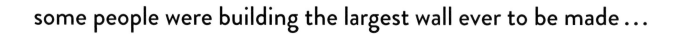

some people were building the largest wall ever to be made...

so they could keep all the other people out.

Meanwhile back on Earth, 5,000 years ago,
people discovered using animals and metal

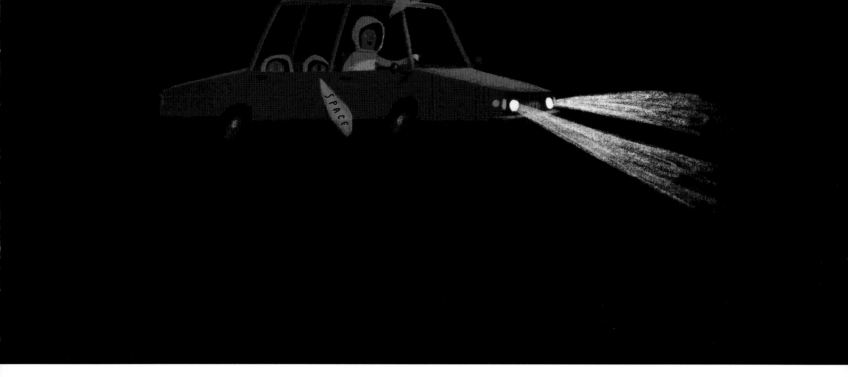

made fighting much more effective.

It's really pretty empty this far out.
It'll take just over 8,000 years to drive to Neptune.

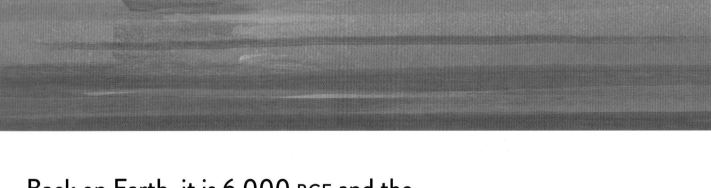

Back on Earth, it is 6,000 BCE and the
sea is still rising from the end of the last Ice Age ...

and early people are fighting
each other with sticks and stones.

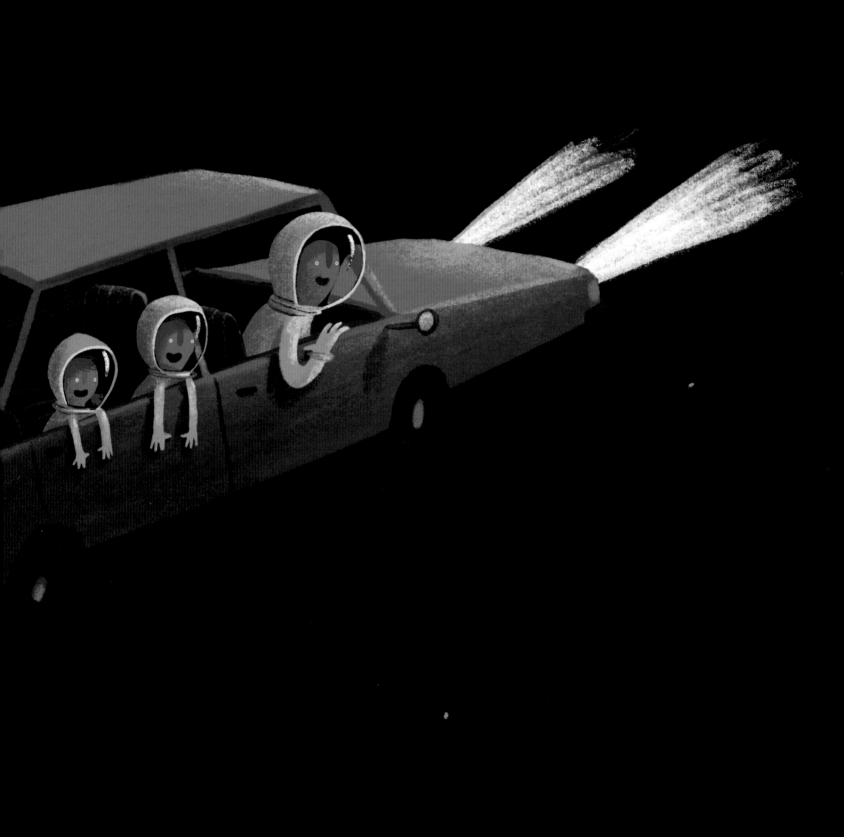

If we carry on,

after driving for 11,000 years, we finally reach Pluto.

there are fewer people on Earth than currently live in Ireland

(around six million) . . .

and they are much too busy surviving
to bother with fighting each other.

Well, that's us. We have reached the end of our solar system

(just one of billions).

Do you want to keep going?

(Next stop: Alpha Centauri, just a seventy-seven-million-year drive away.)

Or,

do you want to go home?

"No matter where you travel, it's always nice to get home."

— **Neil Armstrong,** on returning to Earth on Apollo 11, 1969

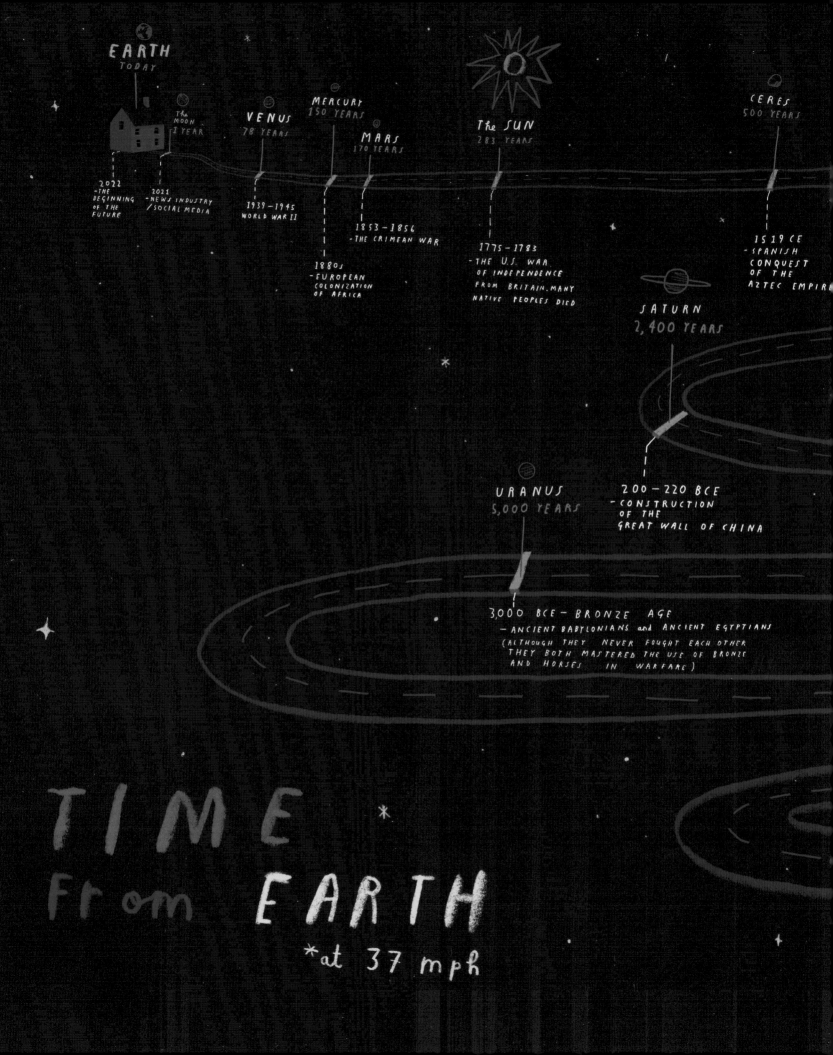